7 SECRET HABITS of SUCCESS

Duane Alley

The 7 Secret Habits of Success

Copyright © 2013 by Duane Alley – http://www.duanealley.com

All rights reserved. No part of this book may be produced or utilised in any form or by any means, electronic or mechanical, including photocopying, recording or by any information storage and retrieval system, without permission in writing from the Publisher.

Published 2013

Publisher: Performance Results Pty Ltd

Graphic Design & Layout: Mélissa Caron – Go-Enki.com
Editor: Richard Burian – Richard-Burian.com

Self Help

ISBN 978-0-9870571-3-6

For my Sister, Danielle Alley.

You're continuing to create

your own success.

TABLE OF CONTENTS

Chapter One – **Focus on Your Outcome** 9

Chapter Two – **Strategic Action** 31

Chapter Three – **Awareness & Attention** 45

Chapter Four – **Flex-ability** 53

Chapter Five – **The Deciding Factor** 61

Chapter Six – **Inner Game of Excellence** 71

Chapter Seven – **Utilisation** 99

Appendix – **The 7 Secret Habits of Success Diagram** 103

01 FOCUS ON YOUR OUTCOME

CHAPTER 1:
FOCUS ON YOUR OUTCOME

> *You've got to know where you're heading if you ever want to arrive."*

Goals, outcomes, dreams, wishes, wants, desires... everyone has them. Whether you know it or not – everyone sets them. Get up, brush teeth, go to work, don't get fired, make a million dollars (before noon), get married, get divorced... whatever they are – they are there. The problem is that many people set and then forget. They want something and then start to focus on everything else other than what they actually want. Or they really do want something but instead of clearly defining what that is, they have some vague and ambiguous idea that leads them exactly nowhere.

The first secret habit of success is simple – *focus on your outcome.*

The first part of this habit is hidden plainly within sight – it is YOUR outcome that you need to focus on. This a point where many people become unstuck. Life today is set up to have us focussed on a lot of things that are actually the priorities of other people – in business even more so. E-mails, phone calls, meetings and social media – they all help us quite literally to keep our sights on other people's priorities and to act for other people's achievements. This is far from being a powerful and effective method of getting what we actually want. Yes, it is true that one way to get what you want is to help as many people as you can to get what they want. But first of all you have to know what it is you really do want in the first place and be okay with getting it now (or in the long run). In my *Performance Mastery Program* I teach that creativity, talent and effort alone will not deliver your results, although a lot of people continue to bang their heads up against the wall thinking this is all there is to it. The true equation is:

This first secret habit is fundamental to you achieving results in life, relationships, health, business or career.

The most fundamental habit to develop here is to begin setting outcomes in everything you do and focus on achieving them. Later we'll talk about how to create and record other goals. First up though, we've just got to get good at actually having them.

Whatever we are doing or going to do comes with an inherent outcome attached to it. Whether you know it or not, it's there. Again, the problem is that unless you were the one who set it, the goal isn't yours. So the answer is to make it so. Make it yours, so you can be sure you are investing your time, effort and energy in places that will take you forward and get you what you actually want.

Start asking the questions:

- ✖ **WHAT DO I WANT FROM THIS?**
- ✖ **WHY AM I DOING THIS?**
- ✖ **WHAT IS THIS GOING TO DO, GET, OR DELIVER?**

Dig down and determine the outcome for every time you are engaged, acting or investing your time. Soon enough you will begin your thoughts with Outcome Focus. You will begin to ask "What do I want" before you start expending time and energy.

Take time right now to determine where your level of Outcome Focus has been over the last week. Fill in the table below for the major "time takers" over the last 7 days. For each major activity or effort you were involved in, list the outcomes that were wanted (if any were set upfront), the results that were achieved (if any were) and if they were actually your outcomes or someone else's priorities.

 The first line has been filled out for you as an example.

MAIN TIME TAKER	OUTCOMES SET	RESULTS ACHIEVED	OUTCOME OWNER
Workplace	Achieve daily targets	80% of target	Boss
MONDAY:			

MAIN TIME TAKER	OUTCOMES SET	RESULTS ACHIEVED	OUTCOME OWNER
TUESDAY:			
WEDNESDAY:			
THURSDAY:			
FRIDAY:			

MAIN TIME TAKER	OUTCOMES SET	RESULTS ACHIEVED	OUTCOME OWNER
SATURDAY:			
SUNDAY:			

Now let's look at the coming week. Below you will find a similar worksheet to the one you just filled in. Look at your week ahead and all the major actions that are scheduled or will need to take place – determine in advance what your top 3 outcomes are for each of the major "time takers":

TOP 3 OUTCOMES
MONDAY:
1. _____
2. _____
3. _____

TOP 3 OUTCOMES TUESDAY:
1. _____
2. _____
3. _____

TOP 3 OUTCOMES WEDNESDAY:
1. _____
2. _____
3. _____

TOP 3 OUTCOMES THURSDAY:
1. _____
2. _____
3. _____

TOP 3 OUTCOMES FRIDAY:
1. _____
2. _____
3. _____

TOP 3 OUTCOMES SATURDAY:
1. _____
2. _____
3. _____

TOP 3 OUTCOMES SUNDAY
1. _____
2. _____
3. _____

You can use the same fundamental thought process and strategy for meetings. I get a lot of requests for meetings, catch-ups and calls. So do many of our Program Members and my personal Coaching and Consulting Clients. They use the same strategy that I employed years ago to ensure every meeting has a purpose and it is in alignment with our own personal goals and outcomes.

Whenever someone asks you for or requests a meeting in any form, ask them for their Top 3 Outcomes (T3s). You can phrase it something like this, "I want to make sure we maximise our time together and I serve you in the best way possible. So, what are the top 3 outcomes/things/priorities you want to achieve from our time together?"

See, the thing is that most people want meetings without knowing this themselves, they just think they need a meeting with you to sort "stuff" out or do "stuff". When you get people around you thinking of their Top 3 Outcomes (T3s) you start to get them focussed. The benefit of this is that you will find that many of the "necessary meetings" become not so important after all – you find you can handle their T3s in an email, phone call or other non-meeting way.

The second part of this strategy is to make sure you inform them of your T3s. This way you are also focussed coming into a meeting. Sometimes of course, you have none – it's their meeting and their outcomes – so just inform them you have no specific outcomes other than to help them achieve theirs. You get much happier people and shorter meetings this way as you all know what's wanted coming in and once it's achieved you can finish and move onto the next priority.

Now to goal setting...

One of the habits of excellence that is innate in many successful people is a want and willingness to set goals and to define their outcomes before any journey.

Without a target to shoot for, the bow, the arrow and even the archer become redundant. When I ask people to write goals out – some have been doing this for a long time, it's almost as natural as breathing. For some though, it is a whole new way of thinking. If it is new for you, then think about it like this... a Goal is nothing more than deciding on and detailing what you want. For decades, I've taught people from 8 to 80 in business all around the world to start with their goal and to define it in the most effective way possible. You might have your own way of writing out your goal. When I share about writing goals, I teach people to write what I call GREATER Goals.

GREATER is an acronym designed to help people craft their outcome in the most effective way possible. I'm going to share it with you here:

- **G - GET REALLY CLEAR ON WHAT YOU WANT**
- **R - REALISTIC**
- **E - END STEP, EVIDENCE & EMOTION**
- **A - AS IF NOW**
- **T - TIMED AND TAKES YOU FORWARD**
- **E - ECOLOGICALLY SOUND**
- **R - REWARD FOR ACHIEVEMENT**

Let me explain them in more detail:

G - GET REALLY CLEAR ON WHAT YOU WANT

Describe what is it you truly want in the most clear and concise way possible. For most people, when they begin to decide what they want to achieve in their future (when they begin to set goals), they describe instead what they don't want. All this does is to focus their minds on not getting something. It's like driving a car by only looking in the rear-view mirror. To start off effectively we must train ourselves to focus instead on what we want. And to get very clear on what that is.

I was teaching a business strategy and leadership training in Los Angeles a few years ago and a participant at the training came to me in the first break of day one and told me they had done many training sessions like this one and had still not produced results they were happy with. I asked them what they wanted and what they were there for. Their response was that they wanted more money in their business. I smiled and reached into my pocket, found a nickel and handed it to them. I then told them to go and deposit that in their business bank account and to pick up their certificate from my training on the way out, because they'd achieved their goal already and they no longer needed to stay. They smiled, and asked me what I meant. I explained that if they wanted 'more' money, they had received it. They definitely wanted something different from 'more', they needed a specific amount. I asked them to think about what that was. How much that was. And I explained that unless they knew precisely what that amount was they had nothing to be aiming at. They came up with a figure and it was a significant amount – a great (or, "greater") goal to shoot for.

I heard from them about three months later; they e-mailed me to say they had achieved that amount and had reset their sights on even greater achievements. They also mentioned that they were a little surprised by how easy it was to achieve something once you knew what that something was.

R – REALISTIC

Setting a goal so big that you honestly know it will never be achievable is not a positive or productive thing to do. Yet, I see so many people doing it for the sake of 'facing their fears'. All this does is to reinforce their own imagined and perceived inadequacies. Instead of throwing yourself up against certain failure only to face the inevitable "I told you so" from that little voice inside your own head... work to build a foundation of 'proof of success'. What I mean is that you want to prove to yourself that you <u>can</u> achieve a goal and furthermore, that when you set a goal, it <u>is</u> possible for you to achieve it.

Here's a simple method to begin with.

If you are someone who has always obtained everything you have ever set your mind to, then go BIG with your goal setting – really challenge yourself. If, however, you are a person who believes you've never actually achieved anything you've ever wanted, then start really, really small. Set yourself some goals that you can be absolutely certain you can achieve. You are training your own subconscious mind now to expect to achieve what you set out to. Over time you will increase the size and complexity of your wants and desires. For the moment, concentrate on proving that you can do it and keep the goals realistic for you. Of course, if you are somewhere in between these two extremes, adjust the strategy accordingly.

E - **END STEP, EVIDENCE & EMOTION**

How will you know you've actually got the goal and furthermore how will you know you've arrived at that place in time. It's all well and good to set down what you want to have happen, but how will you know you've arrived. This is different for everyone. What happens for many people is that they set a goal to achieve something incredible. What they don't do is work out in advance how they will know they have achieved it. When you don't know what your end step is and how you're going to know you've arrived there (what I call 'evidence') you can continue on an endless loop of striving for a goal that you have already achieved when you could have celebrated and moved on to the next thing. Let me give you a real life example. I run a program called *The Inner Game of Everything* on a tropical island resort off the coast of Singapore, on Bintan Island. It is a gorgeous paradise in northern Indonesia.

If you set your goal to attend the training, how will you know you've achieved it – what is the last thing that has to happen so you know it's complete and what has to happen for you to let you know you have arrived at that step? For some, it will be signing the registration form and that's it. They can imagine themselves sitting down with me or one of my Team and filling in a form to attend. For others, it could be jumping on the plane to take them there. Once they sit down and the Captain makes his or her announcement they know they've achieved their goal. And still, for others, they need to step off through the front gates of the resort and be greeted by the resort Team, welcoming them to their island experience. Everyone has a different 'end step' and a unique way of knowing they've arrived.

The third and equally powerful element of this facet of goal setting is the emotion you will feel when you have achieved your outcome. Emotions are a powerful anchor that we can use to lock in the moment of achievement. Our subconscious mind is also the repository of our emotions. In fact it is said that the language of the subconscious is our emotions. When we focus on the emotion we will feel when we achieve our goal, our subconscious can now engage in the process and seek to create that emotion.

A - AS IF NOW

Remember, our subconscious mind accounts for over 90% of our total mind-functioning. It really is the powerhouse driving our achievements. One of the big mistakes people make when setting goals is to talk about what they want to have 'one day', what they 'will get' when they achieve their goal. What they are really doing is programming their subconscious with the fact that they don't have it now.

Here's how it works:

You say, "I want to have X"... subconscious hears, "I don't have X". One of the prime directives of the subconscious mind is to validate what we believe as being true. Its job is to 'make us right'. So, when we program it constantly with the fact that we 'don't have something' our subconscious looks for ways to make this true. There may be many opportunities to get that thing we want, but our beautiful subconscious mind will find ways to make sure we don't get it unless it proves we are wrong.

Instead, you want to talk about what you want as if you have it now. You want to program your subconscious with the fact that your achievement of the goal is real.

There's a commonly taught truth that the subconscious mind cannot tell the difference between reality and a vividly imagined (or habitually programmed) desire. This is true. The conscious mind, on the other hand <u>can</u> and it knows that while you really don't have X but are saying you do, you really don't. This sets up what the achievement experts call "structural tension" in the mind. Your subconscious believes it to be true that you have something and your conscious mind knows you don't. Because both sides of our mind desire and require being in sync, the subconscious rapidly sets about doing everything possible to make sure the conscious can agree that we do have X. It systematically searches for the opportunities and possibilities that will lead to our desired goal.

T - TIMED AND TAKES YOU FORWARD

Another critical distinction that sets apart a wish from a goal is timing. All goals need to have a time stamp placed on them. This helps validate the End Step and Evidence we talked about previously. When talking about what you want it is very important to say when you want that to happen. E.g. "It is now August 29th, 2017" or "It is the end of April this year".

As with the very first step (becoming clear on what you want instead of what you don't), it is important to make sure that the goal you are setting takes you forward and towards the positive outcome. Do not use any negative words or focus on what you don't want. Do not incorporate any "away-from" forms or negatives. Instead, ensure you are only using positive and forward focused language to describe your goal and achievement.

E - ECOLOGICALLY SOUND

Does your goal work to support and serve you? Does it work to serve and support others? Does it work to serve and support the system you are operating in? If the goal is about your family, then does it serve and support your family? If it is in the context of your job, does it serve and support your company or business?

One of the key elements that stops us from achieving our goals and desires is that we realise at some point succeeding will cause pain or trouble to ourselves, others we care about or to the people or environment around us. It is important to ensure we have tackled this issue in advance and set ourselves up for true and lasting success from the get-go. Ensure the realisation of your goal is positive, safe and supportive for you, everyone and everything else involved.

R - REWARD FOR ACHIEVEMENT

What are you going to give yourself as a reward when you get the goal?

One of the major distinctions differentiating what I teach from many others is our focus on reward and celebration. When we teach someone to set a goal we ask them to determine and define the reward they will receive for achieving that goal.

This works almost like positive reinforcement training in children or animals to condition the subconscious mind to conspire for the achievement of your outcomes. When we reward ourselves, we feel good and the subconscious recognises and likes this. We link the reward to the achievement of the goal and pretty soon the subconscious becomes addicted (in a very positive way) to the good feeling of the achievement and reward.

—◇—

EXERCISE

Write down your Top 3 Time Goals from previous sections and then construct Greater Goals to aim for while achieving them.

TOP GOAL #1

G State your goal as clearly and simply as possible. What do you really want?

R Is this aim and achievement realistic for you?   ☐ YES   ☐ NO

E How will you know you've actually got the goal?

| END STEP: | EVIDENCE: | EMOTION: |
| What is the last step you have to do to achieve your goal? | What facts/objects/achievements will show that you have your goal? | What is the last step you have to do to achieve your goal? |

A AS IF NOW: How can you change your language to speak about the future as if it was already true? Rewrite your greater goal into the present tense.

T When do you want that to happen?   ___ / ___ / ___
How will this take you forward?
What future goal will this allow you to start working towards?

E Does your goal work to support and serve you?   ☐ YES   ☐ NO
Does it work to serve and support others?   ☐ YES   ☐ NO

R What are you going to give yourself as a reward when you get the goal?

EXERCISE (CONT.)

TOP GOAL #2

G State your goal as clearly and simply as possible. What do you really want?

R Is this aim and achievement realistic for you?   ☐ YES   ☐ NO

E How will you know you've actually got the goal?

END STEP:	EVIDENCE:	EMOTION:
What is the last step you have to do to achieve your goal?	What facts/objects/achievements will show that you have your goal?	What is the last step you have to do to achieve your goal?

A AS IF NOW: How can you change your language to speak about the future as if it was already true? Rewrite your greater goal into the present tense.

T When do you want that to happen?   ____ / ____ / ____
How will this take you forward? What future goal will this allow you to start working towards?

E Does your goal work to support and serve you?   ☐ YES   ☐ NO
Does it work to serve and support others?   ☐ YES   ☐ NO

R What are you going to give yourself as a reward when you get the goal?

TOP GOAL #3

(G) State your goal as clearly and simply as possible. What do you really want?

(R) Is this aim and achievement realistic for you? ☐ YES ☐ NO

(E) How will you know you've actually got the goal?

END STEP:	EVIDENCE:	EMOTION:
What is the last step you have to do to achieve your goal?	What facts/objects/achievements will show that you have your goal?	What is the last step you have to do to achieve your goal?

(A) AS IF NOW: How can you change your language to speak about the future as if it was already true? Rewrite your greater goal into the present tense.

(T) When do you want that to happen? ___ / ___ / ___

How will this take you forward? What future goal will this allow you to start working towards?

(E) Does your goal work to support and serve you? ☐ YES ☐ NO
Does it work to serve and support others? ☐ YES ☐ NO

(R) What are you going to give yourself as a reward when you get the goal?

Once you have crafted your GREATER Goal in order to create the greatest chance of success it's important to begin speaking about it or 'stating' it in such a way that it causes a subconscious programming of the success. What usually happens when people talk about their 'goals' is they say it in such a way to prove they actually don't have it. For example, people will say, "I want to have a holiday on a tropical island."

What they are really doing is telling the subconscious mind that they don't currently have a holiday and that they just want it. The subconscious mind works in the 'now-reality' and not in the 'future-desire'; so it cannot process the fact that you don't have it but want it — only the truth of the current reality that you do not currently have a holiday.

It is also a primary function of the subconscious to validate beliefs that you hold to be true. Once you 'believe something is real', the subconscious looks for ways to 'prove you right'. So when you tell it you don't have something — whether it be a holiday or a $100,000 contract — it will ensure you don't get it so that you can remain right in your belief.

The only way to overcome this and to use the natural function of your subconscious genius is to state the future desired goal in such a way that the subconscious hears it is a present fact and can then operate on proving your assumption or belief real. That means helping you get it.

By doing this it also creates what achievement experts call "structural tension" whereby the subconscious is being programmed to believe you have something and at the same time the conscious mind knows you don't. This tension can only be resolved by the achievement of the goal. This means your subconscious faculties will work even harder in collusion with your conscious focus to achieve the outcome you desire.

Here's how to do just this...

First we start by stating the goal achievement date in the present and positive, for example, "It is now August 27, 2014...". You put in whatever day and date you are setting as your goal.

Then you add what I call your emotional hook — that is the emotion you will feel when you achieve this thing you want. As emotions can only be felt in the present moment (that is you can't feel excited soon, you can only feel excited when you feel excited), this emotional statement creates a beacon for your subconscious mind to latch onto and helps focus it on the present moment you will experience in the future.

Example: "It is now August 27, 2014 and I am feeling excited..."

Third it is now time to state the end step/evidence procedure for your achievement, "It is now August 27, 2014 and I am feeling excited as I am walking through the entrance to Club Med to join *The Inner Game of Everything* experience with a group of amazing and inspirational people".

THE BASIC STRUCTURE IS:

> **IT IS NOW**
> (The achievement date.)

> **I FEEL**
> (Add your emotional state when you arrive here.)

> **I AM**
> (What is your evidence procedure? Where are you and what are you doing?)

> **I HAVE**
> (What is the end step of your goal that tells you have achieved it?)

—◇—

02 STRATEGIC ACTION

CHAPTER 2:
STRATEGIC ACTION

> *Nothing worth having is not worth doing to get."*

Once you've got the target in sight the most important thing you can do to make sure you get it is do something. You need to act not soon, but now.

You've got your outcome sorted and you know what you want... the most important thing you can ever do at this or any other point in time is DOING. There has never been a goal achieved, money made, success created or dream attained without action taking place. I say in my programs and trainings that ACTION is the one key necessary to any ACHIEVEMENT.

This is true... but action without a strategy is wasted. You can expend all the efforts climbing the tallest ladder, but when you find out it's leaning against the wrong wall (or worse it's not even the right ladder) you're not going to get what you want. In fact you'll get a whole lot of aggravation, agitation and annoyance because you'll either need to give up or start all over again.

Isaac Newton's First Law of Motion states that an object that is in motion stays in motion, while an object at rest will stay at rest, unless it is acted on by an external force. This is why many guru-teachers will say that any action is better than none. I have known the pain of taking action for the sake of not sitting still before and had to then completely reverse everything I had done and undo a lot of mistakes that didn't need to happen if only I had been a little more strategic about what I was doing.

During an interview I was listening to once I heard a business strategist get asked if there was one thing he thought he could distil his knowledge down to in order to help every business person in the world what would it be. The answer was simple and profound, "Do the right things." The interviewer laughed, thinking it was a joke and went on to the next question. The strategist was right though; there are many things that could be done and doing is necessary but which are the right ones.

Here's a strategy that I call "*Back To Now*" or BTN.

First, a story... have you ever been on a trip somewhere, say a road trip where it took a very long time to get to your destination, but when it was time to turn around and go home it seemed to take a ridiculously short time to get back, to actually reach home? I bet you have. I've yet to meet someone who has not had a similar experience at some time in their life. Imagine if we could apply that "magic" to achieving your desired outcomes.

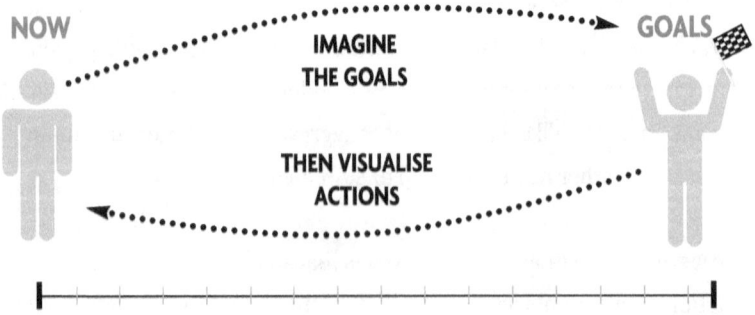

That's where my BTN Strategy comes in.

1. You've already set your outcome and following the GREATER Goals system you know what your End Step & Evidence will be that tells you you've achieved your aims. What I want you to do is imagine being in that time in your life right now. Imagine you have achieved the outcome and you're ready to celebrate that win.

2. Take a piece of paper and at the bottom of it write down the End Step and Evidence for achieving the outcome.

3. Now, imagine yourself at that time. What was the thing that had to happen immediately before you reached the End Step? What was the thing that had to happen that led to the inevitable achievement of the goal?

4. Take your paper again and just above where you wrote the End Step and Evidence for achieving the outcome, write in that thing that needed to happen.

5. Now, what was the major objective, land mark or milestone that needed to be achieved before you reached that last step?

6. Take paper – write it down.

7. Keep working backwards towards the starting point and write down each necessary action, effort, milestone or objective that needed to happen.

8. Eventually you will reach right now; sitting down and writing this list or strategy.

9. It is time to turn yourself around now that you know the road map ahead and start the real journey toward achieving your outcome; this time it'll be a shorter trip because you already know the terrain and path ahead.

GOAL #1

WHAT NEEDS TO HAPPEN? _____

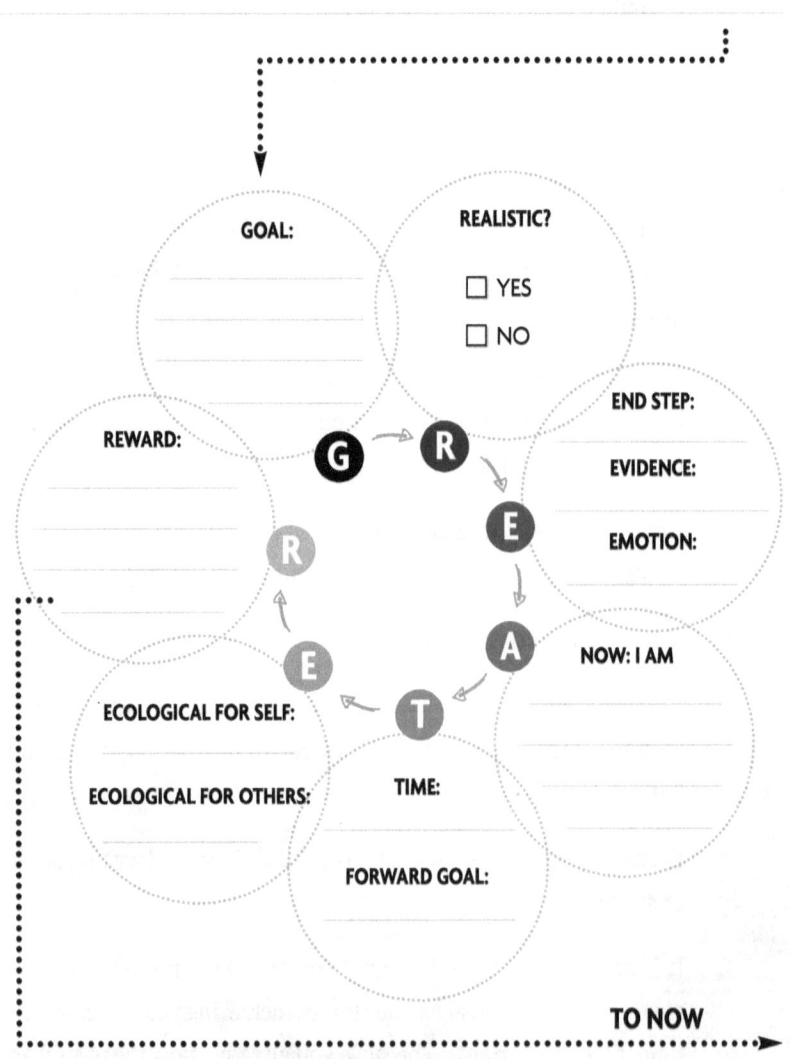

NOW

IMAGINE THE GOAL AS IF NOW: _____
_____
_____
_____

- **EVIDENCE:**
- **STEP BEFORE END STEP:**
- **STEP BEFORE THAT:**
- **END STEP:**
- **STEP BEFORE THAT:**
- **MAJOR MILESTONE:**
- **STEP BEFORE THAT:**
- **STEP BEFORE THAT:**

TO NEXT GOAL →

7 Secret Habits of Success — Duane Alley

GOAL #2

WHAT NEEDS TO HAPPEN? _____
_____
_____

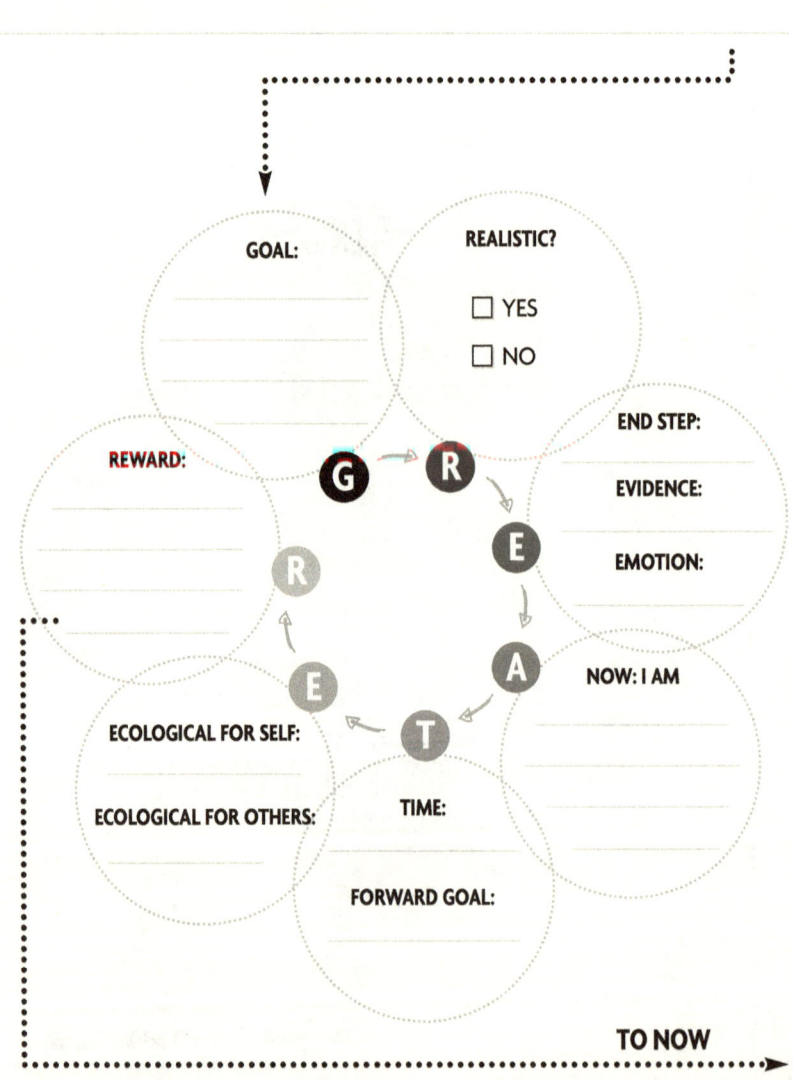

NOW

IMAGINE THE GOAL AS IF NOW: _____

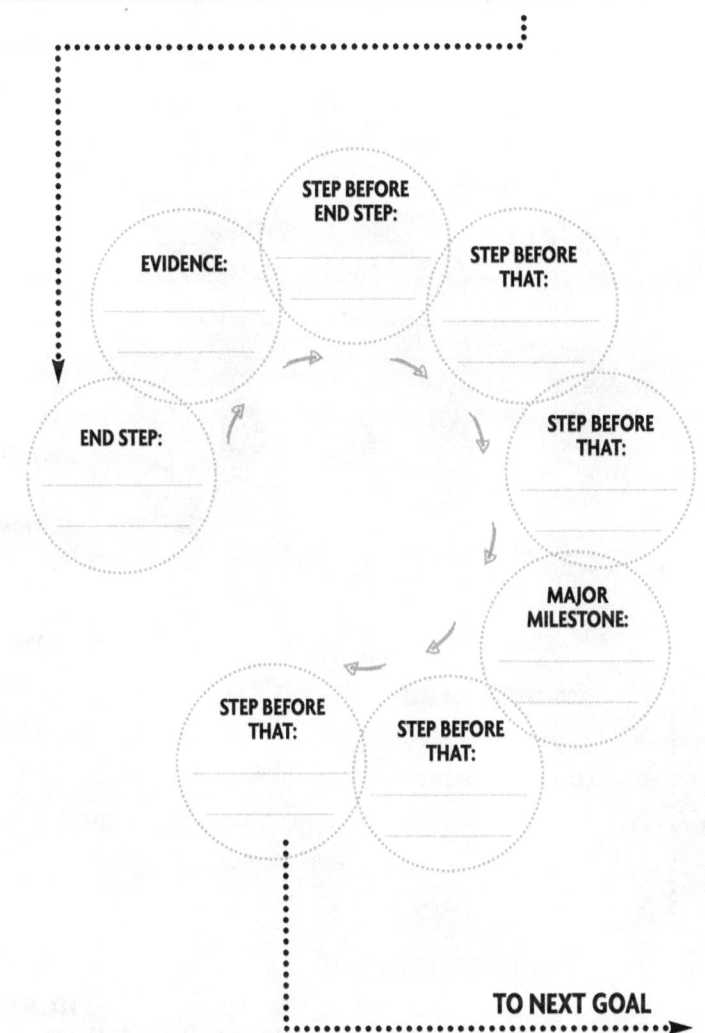

TO NEXT GOAL

GOAL #3

WHAT NEEDS TO HAPPEN? _____
_____
_____

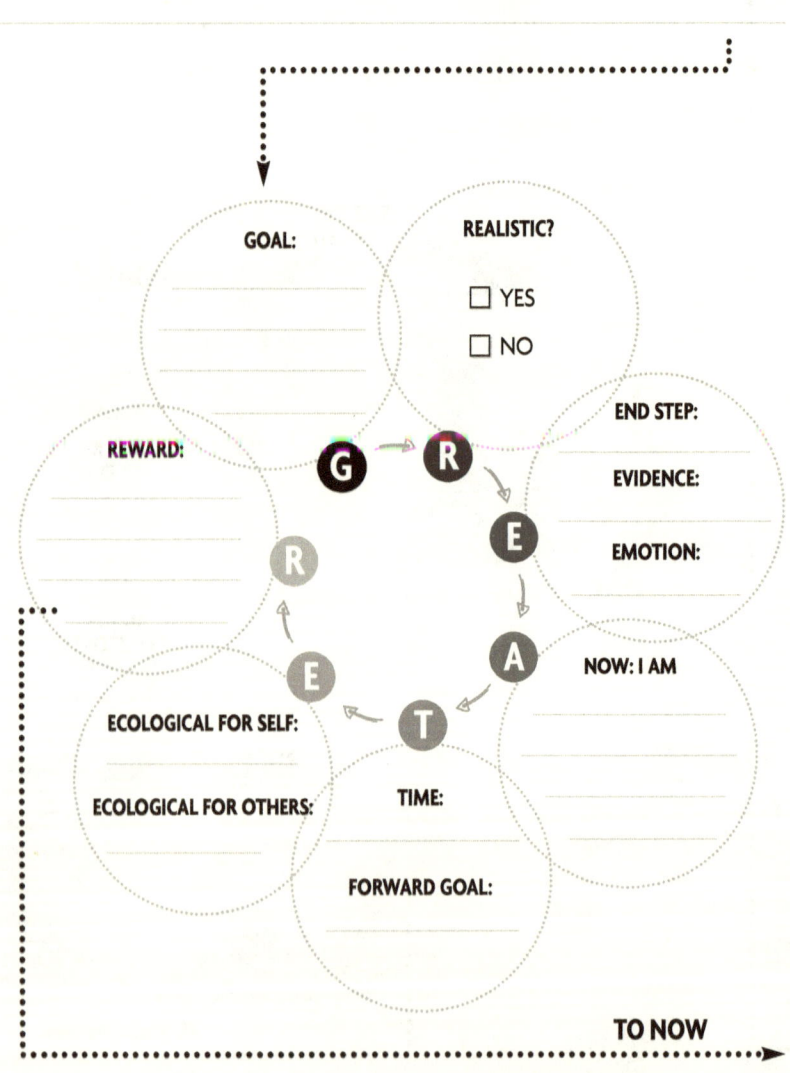

NOW

IMAGINE THE GOAL AS IF NOW:

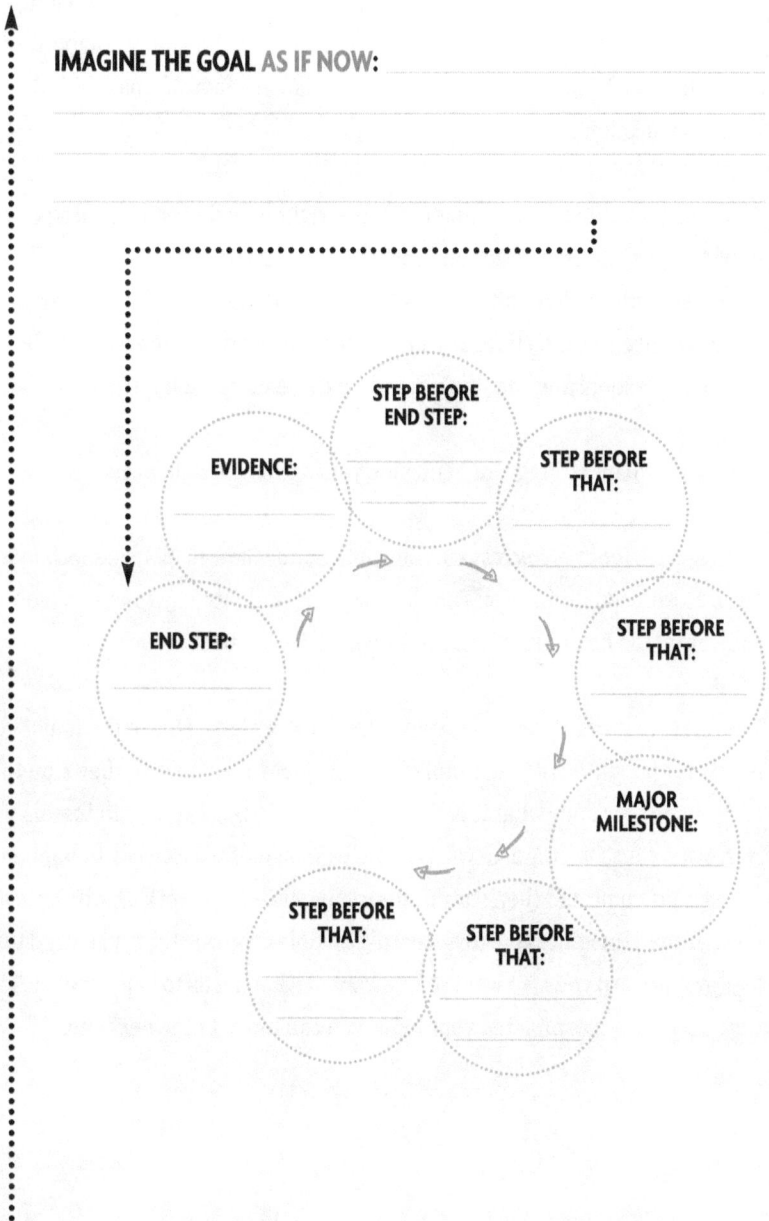

Sometimes when faced with a result you want to achieve that seems a long way off it is easy to become overloaded, overwhelemed and confused about what action to take. When I face situations like this I ask myself what I call the 'No Excuses Question'.

"No excuses... What is one thing I could do right now that will create a positive impact on my desired result and move me toward its achievement?". There's always something that pops into my head and something will also occur to you when you use this question. If you get stuck in the next exercise, use the 'No Excuses Question' and then go out and do those things you identify.

This is a brilliant strategy for achieving your goals and outcomes.

The *7 Secret Habits of Success* are about integrating these habits at a subconscious level. Here's something you can do every day and any day to ensure you are cultivating the habit of Strategic Action in all that you do.

The strategy is called N^2 and it stands for 'Now & Next'. One of the major stall points for people achieving is not knowing what to do 'now' so they stop their progress to work out what it is they need to be doing. The way to fix this is to start with your Outcome, develop a strategic plan of what needs to happen to get your outcome and then start putting your strategy to work. Do the first step now. At the same time you are focussing on doing the one thing you need to do to <u>move forward</u> you also want to be aware of what needs to happen next. That way, once you've completed your 'now' you can move to the next one.

—◇—

 **EXERCISE**

Take a good look at your top priorities at the moment and determine what is the first NOW you need to do in order to <u>move forward</u> on the project and what is the next.

Do that for your top 3 projects below and then plan time to get to work on them.

 The first line has been filled out for you as an example.

TOP PRIORITY #1	DO WHAT NOW	DO WHAT NEXT	TIME
Lose 20 kg	Go for a walk	Plan and implement balanced diet and exercise routine	2-3 workouts per week 30 minute walk every day 6 months

💡 EXERCISE (CONT.)

TOP PRIORITY #2	DO WHAT NOW	DO WHAT NEXT	TIME

TOP PRIORITY #3	DO WHAT NOW	DO WHAT NEXT	TIME

03 AWARENESS & ATTENTION

CHAPTER 3:
AWARENESS & ATTENTION

> *A rock pile ceases to be a rock pile the moment a single man contemplates it, bearing within him the image of a cathedral."*
>
> **- Antoine de Saint-Exupery**

So far you've set your Outcome and you are focussed on what you want to have, achieve or create. You are also starting to take action because you know that nothing will happen without it. The key now... the third secret habit of success is to actually be aware of what is going on, to pay attention to whether what you are doing is actually producing the result you want and intend. You've got to be aware of what's going on and the environment it's all happening in. Aware of the actions you are taking and the results they are producing.

If something isn't working the best time to notice this is when it starts to not work, not when the whole project derails.

There is so much going on all the time; actions being taken, reactions occurring. Training yourself to be aware of what is happening around you and how that is impacting your plans and efforts as well as how your efforts and actions are impacting others is a secret habit of success.

When I worked at McDonald's and was training to be a Manager in my late teens and early 20s we were taught to "manage the store with all our senses". We were taught to not only 'look' at what was going on but to also be aware of our other senses and what information we could get from them. To be aware of sounds, touch, taste and smell as each of these senses can deliver vital information that could prevent minor and major problems as well as alert you to opportunities to maximise. This is a strategy and understanding that I have taken with me through every job, career and business I have ever had. It has allowed me to not just accidently stumble onto problems to fix but rather to proactively monitor all activities to ensure fires were extinguished at the ember stage well before raging inferno level.

In neuro-linguistic programming and the coaching sciences, this skill is known as sensory acuity. It is the purposeful use of all senses to glean information that is useful and determine how a coaching client is being affected by your work with them.

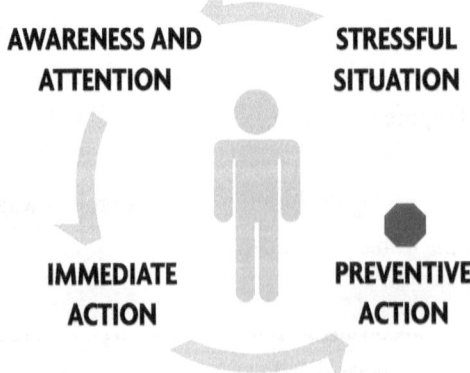

There is another related element to this capacity of increased awareness and that is what in coaching I call 'situational attention'. Increasing your awareness allows you to be alerted to things you might not normally realise. Situational Attention is the ability to relate the context of the situation to your awareness or sensory input. You may become aware of more information and in different situations that input will mean different things. The same actions in different people will likewise indicate different situations. In the movie, *The Bourne Identity*, the protagonist, Jason Bourne is sitting in a roadside restaurant and talking to his travelling companion. He has lost his memory of who he is and cannot understand why as he looks at the room he is noticing things in a very different way from 'normal' people. His companion sees a room of diners and various vehicles outside. Jason Bourne, who at this stage does not know he is actually a trained Special Forces operative and expert assassin, describes the 'lines of sight', threats, available weapons and his acute awareness of his own physical endurance at the precise altitude and environmental conditions. He is demonstrating his own Situational Attention. When we take in the increased information in awareness we must also evaluate the situation in order to know what to pay attention to and how to do it.

We can build these dual capacities through two very simple daily habits. In changing the way you perceive and interact with others and your environment in simple ways, you will begin to develop an augmented skill in other areas of your businesses and life.

First:
Something very simple. Every time you hear someone sneeze, say, "bless you". Forget the superstitions behind this custom. Focus instead on your increasing awareness and recognition of what's happening around you. Even if you don't say it aloud, say it to yourself.

Second:

A little harder. And there are two parts to this one. One for those of you who drive a car or ride a motorbike and the other for those of you who don't (or drivers can do this too). Begin to become even more aware of what other drivers want to do. Notice if people want to change lanes and simply let them in. It's about noticing and acting on what you notice. You can do the same if you are walking in the street. This is even more powerful in training your awareness and attention, particularly when doing this in busy streets or shopping malls. Go about your business as usual and allow yourself to become aware to others, their actions and apparent wants. Respond to them so that you can navigate busy thoroughfares effortlessly. Pay attention to the behaviour of others and you will begin to pre-empt their next actions. It's not really magic; it's just paying enough attention and engaging your full awareness to fully take in your surroundings.

—◇—

💡 EXERCISE

In the first column, write down a situation you are usually stressed in which you would like to change your attitude with. In the second column, write down what you need to be aware of in your environment and what your senses should be paying attention to; write down what annoys you the most about this situation. Then write down the immediate action you can take to snap you out of your bad feelings. Finally, write a preventive action that you can take in future the situation entirely.

 The first line has been filled out for you as an example.

SITUATION #1	TO BE AWARE OF	ACTION	PREVENTIVE ACTION
The road is blocked by construction & you are starting to be upset	You don't like being in situations you can't control	Turn the car around and find an alternate route	Check road reports before leaving for work

EXERCISE (CONT.)

SITUATION #2	TO BE AWARE OF	ACTION	PREVENTIVE ACTION

SITUATION #3	TO BE AWARE OF	ACTION	PREVENTIVE ACTION

04 FLEX-ABILITY

CHAPTER 4:
FLEX-ABILITY

> *"If you notice it isn't working then it's got to change."*

Flex-ability of behaviour is the ingredient that will ensure you always win.

First you have set your outcome and continue to hold it in focus to ensure your success. You have taken action as the key to your achievement and you are paying increased attention and have become more aware of what is happening, what is working and what isn't.

The next logical step and fourth secret habit of success is your own flex-ability; in particular your behavioural flex-ability. This is the ability to choose to behave in different ways when what you are doing isn't working. It is often said that the person who has the most flex-ability of behaviour is the person who controls the system. Think about this for a minute, many parents will tell you that although they really want to be the one in control, it is often their children that really rule the roost.

Have you ever seen a child having a tantrum in a shop? The child is stomping their feet, holding their breath, pounding their fists and screaming for that toy that they have to have right now or the world will end. The parent can usually do nothing but try to quiet their child. Initially they deny the request from their child who a moment ago was a little angel and is now rapidly transforming into a fire-breathing monster. After many tears and multiple failed attempts to say 'no' and get the kid away from the offending toys the parent finally gives in and says 'yes'. At this stage the tears disappear (from the child) and they say thank you and happily skip toward the register. Nearly every parent I know has been there and still shudders as they remember the last time. Who's in control of this situation? Obviously, the kid. They are able to completely transform their behaviour in order to create a result they want and can swing easily from placid to torrid and all the way to smiling again. The parent only has one way to react… and that doesn't work.

What's something else that could work? Simple, as a parent the only way to 'win' in this situation is to have more behavioural flex-ability than the child. When the child starts the tantrum expecting an argument and eventual surrender… here's what I have done in the past and it worked. Their lip starts to quiver and I make mine quiver as well. As they start their demands, I fall to the ground and pound my fist showing them an even bigger 'hissy fit' than the child had ever seen. At this time, the tears disappeared and their voice dropped to a whisper and I was told, "Umm, OK. Sorry, are you, okay? We don't have to get the toy? Come on… you're embarrassing me. OK already. Let's go." Parental crisis averted through a powerful use of behavioural flex-ability.

This isn't a lesson in parenting, although if you are a parent or are ever in a position like this… give it a try. Thank me later.

Even with the first three secret habits of success in place it is possible for this train to derail if you are more concerned about how you are doing something than what you want to achieve. Remember, you must first and foremost be focussed on Outcome. In business and life, too many people lock themselves into their 'outlook' instead. It's their 'way' or the highway. Instead you must realise there are always multiple ways to achieve any outcome.

—◇—

EXERCISE

The following exercise will help you engrain these habits of success in your life so that you can focus first and foremost on your Outcome. You should do the exercise three times, one action plan to engrain these habits in the three top priorities of your life.

GOAL #1

1 What is your Goal / Outcome?

2 How are you going to achieve this?

List the first few steps.

1.

2.

3.

3 How else can you achieve the same result or better?

List 3 alternative routes you can take to your outcome.

1.

2.

3.

 **EXERCISE (CONT.)**

GOAL #2

1 What is your Goal / Outcome?

2 How are you going to achieve this?

List the first few steps.

1.
2.
3.

3 How else can you achieve the same result or better?

List 3 alternative routes you can take to your outcome.

1.
2.
3.

GOAL #3

1 What is your Goal / Outcome?

2 How are you going to achieve this?

List the first few steps.

1.

2.

3.

3 How else can you achieve the same result or better?

List 3 alternative routes you can take to your outcome.

1.

2.

3.

05 THE DECIDING FACTOR

CHAPTER 5:
THE DECIDING FACTOR

> *Decide,*
> *Get Determined,*
> *and Do it...*
> *it's that simple."*

And it really is... that simple. The problem is, no matter how simple this 3-step strategy is, nothing happens without the decision to start off the whole process.

A key secret habit of the successful is the ability and capacity to make decisions. Having spent nearly two decades studying success and successful people from all areas, industries and countries and in every level of social, economic and business achievement I have discovered one important aspect of their achievement is their ability and capacity to make decisions very quickly, firmly and change their mind only when they need to. On the other hand, 'un-successful' people will avoid decisions wherever possible and when they are forced to make any form of decision, they will also falter and change their mind rapidly and repeatedly.

Your ability and willingness to be decisive in and of itself isn't the sole factor of creating success. By making decisions quickly you increase the speed that people are able to get to action. When decisions take a long time to make, this holds up all the other 'secret habits'. It isn't possible to get to action when you don't know what you want to do – in fact it isn't possible to focus on your outcome when you haven't decided what that is.

A great teacher and friend of mine, Kevin Nations (who happens to be one of the most influential, intelligent and successful trainers of sales and sales people I have ever met and I truly do believe in the world), says when having a conversation with any Client or sales prospect that he is not after them saying 'yes' or even 'no'. All he wants from them is a decision. He teaches that it is the lack of ability to make a decision that holds more people back than nearly any other malady when it comes to business and achievement.

When I teach sales trainings I encourage sales people to go to the phones or meetings with one objective in mind – to get a decision. When they do this they will get more "yes" responses than they ever thought possible. If they simply go after a 'yes' they will be terrified by the number of 'no's' they achieve.

Across human history, people have always had to make decisions. For millennia, it has meant the difference between collapse, survival and abundant survival. In modern times, this ability has waned. Mass media, marketing and our increasingly consumer-influenced lifestyle has created a deepening social hypnosis coercing us to pass our decision making power to someone or something else. To put it plainly, we are out of practise at making decisions. We have come to believe it is too hard to make our own full decisions, too difficult to take control of what we want and need. This also means we must take responsibility for our own lives and achievements.

The first element of recovering our strength of decision-making is to just start making them again. How many times do you yourself or perhaps hear others get asked what they'd like for dinner, which movie to watch, what restaurant to visit... and the answer is something like, "Not sure – you choose"; "I don't care, what do you want to do?" or the like. These seem like small issues and items to concern ourselves with but learning to take charge of these small decisions again leads directly to rediscovering and recovering our ability to make the bigger choices and ultimately those massive and master-decisions in life.

I first started sharing this concept of Recovering Decision-Making during our Life & Destiny Private Retreat events in Australia. In one of the very first events of this kind that I ran, a couple was attending. These are amazing people, great friends and now Members in our advanced programs. We'll call them Jason and Lee-Anne (because those are their names). During the pre-event dinner meeting I watched a lot of interactions where each was giving their own Decision-Making Power over to the other with questions and answers like I've written about above. During the Retreat Event I shared this idea and the change in both of them was immediate. At every lunch and dinner for the entire weekend, they stopped seeking permission from the other or validation of their own wants and began making fast and firm decisions on what they truly desired.

This minor change brought about a range of deeper changes and more pervasive shifts in their personal, home and business lives. Both Jason and Lee-Anne began to step up to the plate read to swing their bat the way they wanted. I spoke with both of them a month or so later and they told me the bigger decisions had become so much easier to make. Many of the large choices at home and in business they'd been delaying on and simply not making a decision about were now in progress as they couldn't stand to just wait for someone else to decide and to therefore control their lives. They were firmly in control. Nearly two years have passed at the time of writing this book and their lives are immensely different now to where they were then. Clearly, this shift to Recover their own decision-making power was not the only change; I do believe though that without this fundamental in place, Jason and Lee-Anne would not have been able to build their success to the level they have and will continue to do so into the future.

START WITH THE SMALL STUFF

From this moment on, for the next 30 days whenever you are called upon or asked to make any form of decision (particularly the small choices) make one – it's that simple. Catch yourself if you find yourself uttering the words, "I don't care" or "You choose" or "Surprise me" (or anything else that means you are giving away your right and willingness to decide for yourself). Even if you don't really care, choose a path and go with it. By doing this we begin to train ourselves to make decisions when called upon to do so. We feed and nurture the belief that we deserve to be able to make the decisions and are worthy of actually getting what we want.

—◇—

💡 EXERCISE

Think about the patterns in your life where you pass over your decision making power.

List below the common times you would "give it away" and decide in advance your desired action. You can do this every day for a week and begin to notice, write down and work out new ways you can take that decision-making power back in your life.

 The first line has been filled out for you as an example.

DAY	SITUATION	OLD HABIT	NEW ACTION
	When people ask what tea I'd like.	"I don't mind, you decide."	Make a choice and stay with it.
MONDAY	1.		
	2.		
	3.		

EXERCISE (CONT.)

DAY	SITUATION	OLD HABIT	NEW ACTION
TUESDAY	1.		
	2.		
	3.		
WEDNESDAY	1.		
	2.		
	3.		

DAY	SITUATION	OLD HABIT	NEW ACTION
THURSDAY	1.		
	2.		
	3.		
FRIDAY	1.		
	2.		
	3.		

EXERCISE (CONT.)

DAY	SITUATION	OLD HABIT	NEW ACTION
SATURDAY	1.		
	2.		
	3.		
SUNDAY	1.		
	2.		
	3.		

06 INNER GAME OF EXCELLENCE

CHAPTER 6:
INNER GAME OF EXCELLENCE

> *It is all to plan; and the plan is good."*

The sixth Secret Habit of Success, which brings all the others together, is always playing an Inner Game of Excellence. Success and Achievement isn't just an outside job. The more strategies we have to create and perform well doesn't necessarily mean the more great results we accomplish.

Sure, playing a "great game" in the outside world of strategies, actions and tangible results is critical to performing at your highest and it's also necessary to ensure your Inner Game is at its peak as well. There's no point studying golf for 20 years and turning up to a basketball game wondering why you're not winning. It's important to ensure your inner game is in alignment with your outer strategies to create true success. The Inner Game of Excellence has two components. The first of these are what I call the Power of Focus.

THE POWER OF FOCUS

Have you ever been in a situation (or heard of one) where the people involved all have a different recollection of what actually went on? This happens a lot when Police take witness statements of incidents and all of the various people involved don't seem to even agree on the fundamental facts of what occurred.

Or maybe been to a party or social event where people described it completely differently to how you experienced it later? Perhaps you thought the party was a great success where everyone had a brilliant time and later on other people at the party told you they thought it was a total disaster filled with people having a terrible experience.

How does this happen? Simple – different people focussed on different things. What we focus on not only affects our experience but creates it.

Years ago, I took my Mother and Grandmother on their first overseas adventure. It was a round-the-world trip. I was teaching in three different countries over a period of six weeks and neither Mum nor Nana had travelled outside of Australia before. During our preparation for the journey, Mum told me that my Nana had asked some other relatives (who had been to Europe) for advice. They told her to avoid Venice and also that Paris was incredibly boring and full of long lines and rude people. Now, Venice and Paris are two of my favourite places on Earth and both were key destinations for our adventure; I was very concerned that Nana might get a negative impression before we even left. I asked her why these relatives had said this and what was Nana's response? Mum told me that they had said Venice was awful because it smelled and you can't even get a good pizza there and that Paris was full of long lines and rude people because they'd gone to The Louvre to see the Mona Lisa but there was a line, it was long so they'd left without even seeing it.

I was shocked. I'd been to both Venice and Paris a number of times and loved every one. Sure, sometimes when the streets flood a little in Venice it can be smelly, but the roads are canals and the place is magical. Pizza? You can get bad pizza anywhere and many of the food stores around the well-beaten tourist routes in Venice are not the highest of quality; but get off the beaten track a little and "go local" and wonders await. Then to Paris, yes there are sometimes big crowds to see the Mona Lisa (or any of the other most famous artworks at The Louvre) but while you are waiting you are surrounded by some of the richest beauty ever created and the wait is worth it when you are able to view some of the most famous creations of the modern or ancient world.

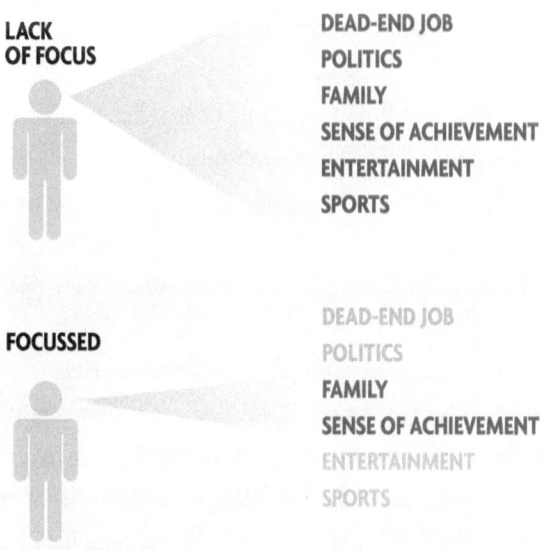

The difference wasn't the events, but rather a difference in focus. When I asked my Nana if she was still excited about the trip she answered, "Of course". I asked her about the comments she had heard from 'the others' and she told me that she wasn't going to listen to that, rather she preferred my stories about those places; my version sounded way better and she was looking forward to *my* Venice and *my* Paris. She also told me that she thought the others were "looking for the bad" and she wasn't going to make the same mistake. I guess she got The Power of Focus naturally. By the way, she had an amazing time and even though she'd only just been released from hospital following a hip replacement, she traipsed all over Italy, France, the U.S. and the U.K. and loved every moment of it.

What's the key here? What we focus on doesn't create the situation; it dictates *our experience* of it. Choose to focus on the negative and disempowering and that is what you will find at every turn. Instead, look out for the positive and affirming and you will be gifted and blessed with exactly this. It's important to realise this won't stop the 'bad stuff' happening; you will however be far better equipped to deal with whatever comes along.

I mentioned earlier that the Inner Game of Excellence has two components. The second is what I call the Gift of Gratitude.

THE GIFT OF GRATITUDE

This Gift of Gratitude is a very special type of focus and it truly is a gift for each of us. It is also a choice that we can make moment to moment. We get to decide to choose to see the blessing in the situations that happen *to* us. It is not only a choice to see the positive though, but rather to be active in our appreciation on that positive and the flow on affect it can, will and does have on our lives and the lives of those around us. Let me give you an exact example.

Literally moments ago... for me... See, I am writing this chapter on a flight from Perth to my home of Brisbane, Australia. I have been teaching my *Patterns of Power Training* to a wonderful group of people for the last few days. The flight attendant just came by to take our orders for lunch. When I ordered the roast chicken salad, she informed me that they didn't have any more and asked if I would like sausages. Now, I don't eat any red meats at all so the answer to the 'sausages question' was a no. On top of that, nearly every other menu choice involved some sort of red meat so all of a sudden I was limited to carrot soup and... well, carrot soup. For about five minutes I was bemoaning the matter in my mind. I've booked and paid for a business class ticket and I couldn't even get a meal that I could eat because after serving less than a dozen Customers before me, they had now run out. I wasn't in a very happy place – in fact I stopped writing for a while just to have a little temper tantrum in my own head.

Then I stopped.

And I thought for a moment about where I was and why I was there as well as what I was doing.

I was on a plane flying across the country after having been in another city teaching people an amazing training that they had taken time out and paid for to come simply to listen to me teach and spend time with me sharing my work with them. Some had driven for hours to be there and others had flown in from overseas just to be at this training. On top of that, I was sitting at the pointy end of the plane, casually writing my next book that many of my Students and Clients had pre-ordered and were eagerly awaiting publication. A little over a decade ago I could not have even imagined being in 'business class', let alone flying all over the country. I'd been working in a job I tolerated and had little on my horizon except tomorrow. Now I own several successful businesses and get to teach *my* trainings all over the world helping people master their own performance and improve their own lives. I'd just been in a city in front of an audience of raving fans and sold out of all of my own current books and CD programs. I was overcome with gratitude for the blessings in my life and all of a sudden the lack of 'chicken salad' didn't matter as much (or at all).

To top it all off, at that point I decided (with a big smile) to start writing again and as I reopened my computer I took special note of the chapter I had not previously realised I was up to – can you guess? Yes, it was this part – Gratitude.

A moment ago I was ridiculously stressed... now I'm feeling immensely blessed. That is the Gift of Gratitude.

I want you to experience this on a tangible basis. Right now, I want you to write. In the space below, I want you to divide your life (that you have lived so far) into 3 equal segments from birth and young childhood right up to today. In each of the chapters of your life I want you to list the 3 major "Stresses" you experienced. What was the 'bad stuff' that happened to or for you? Then in the column beside it, think through and search for the "Blessings" you have received because of what you thought was 'bad' at the time. Every 'bad' or what we sometimes call 'negative' moment in our lives is only so because we are yet to identify the positive connection or blessing to have come from it. Certainly, this does not take away from those times we wish would never have happened or suddenly make those times of sorrow or loss sweet and nice. As I remember my Father's death now it is still incredibly painful and a point of grief for me. At the time, I was not looking for blessings other than the fact that I was able to share life with him for the 21 years I had. Now, though and for many years I have come to realise and appreciate all the positives and blessings that have transpired or come to me, my Family and others because of the growth, changes and learning that happened due to his passing.

Fill out the following chart that segments your life into three sections. Write down in the first column the major stress or negative event and then the blessing or point of gratitude that you got from it:

FIRST THIRD OF LIFE (from Birth to _____)

MAJOR STRESS OR NEGATIVE EVENT	BLESSING / POINT OF GRATITUDE
1.	
2.	
3.	
4.	
5.	
6.	
7.	
8.	
9.	
10.	
11.	
12.	

SECOND THIRD OF LIFE (from _____ to _____)

MAJOR STRESS OR NEGATIVE EVENT	BLESSING / POINT OF GRATITUDE
1.	
2.	
3.	
4.	
5.	
6.	
7.	
8.	
9.	
10.	
11.	
12.	

THIRD THIRD OF LIFE (from _____ to Today)

MAJOR STRESS OR NEGATIVE EVENT	BLESSING / POINT OF GRATITUDE
1.	
2.	
3.	
4.	
5.	
6.	
7.	
8.	
9.	
10.	
11.	
12.	

I believe that everything does happen for a reason and that reason ultimately serves us; in fact I have a saying that, *"It is all to plan; and the plan is good."* It's just sometimes we aren't far enough away from the dark time or have not been able to look deeply enough into it to fully realise and appreciate the blessing and therefore be grateful for it. Mother Teresa was quoted once as saying, "I know God only gives me what I can handle; I just wish he didn't trust me as much as he does".

As you begin to make the connection and appreciate the Gift of Gratitude in your life, you are poised for more abundance and achievement than ever before. It is important though that the Gift of Gratitude not just become one 'momentary' spark but rather a habit of excellence that will continue to bring ongoing success and inspiration.

For the next 31 days I invite you to do this. On waking in the morning think of and list 3 things, people or moments you are most grateful for in your whole life. Then before going to bed at night, list 3 moments, people or events you are especially grateful for from that day. Set an alarm on your phone or post a reminder somewhere you will see it to do this so that you have your moment for the Gift of Gratitude for Life in the morning before launching into the day and for this Day in the evening before sleeping that night. I know this will enhance your life beyond explanation.

I have included a journal for this on the next page – bookmark this section and come back to it daily for the next 31 days. This is something I encourage Clients and Students to take up as a life-long habit. After the next 31 days you might like to create a special journal just for this purpose. To help you a bit, I have created a six-month companion to this text called the *Gift of Gratitude Journey*. This journal will help you identify your great gratitudes for a whole half a year. Not only will it keep you focussed on being grateful, but will help you cement in the new way of thinking just by doing the exercises on a daily basis.

—◇—

 **EXERCISE**

Below you have a journal that you can use for 31 days. Every morning, list the three things in your life from the past that you are grateful for. Then, in the evening before going to sleep, list the three things you are grateful for from that day. List anything you want from every area of your life and do it for 31 days.

 The first line has been filled out for you as an example.

31 DAYS GIFT OF GRATITUDE JOURNAL

	MORNING	EVENING
EXAMPLE *Today, I am grateful for:*	1. My family and their love 2. Opportunity to work where I do 3. Living in such an incredible country	Beautiful sunrise this morning Amazing service from the Starbucks Partner New Member coming into our program
DAY 1 *Today, I am grateful for:*	1. 2. 3.	

EXERCISE (CONT.)

	MORNING	EVENING
DAY 2 *Today, I am grateful for:*	1. 2. 3.	
DAY 3 *Today, I am grateful for:*	1. 2. 3.	

	MORNING	EVENING

DAY 4

Today, I am grateful for:

1.

2.

3.

DAY 5

Today, I am grateful for:

1.

2.

3.

EXERCISE (CONT.)

	MORNING	EVENING
DAY 6 *Today, I am grateful for:*	1. 2. 3.	
DAY 7 *Today, I am grateful for:*	1. 2. 3.	

	MORNING	EVENING

DAY 8

Today, I am grateful for:

1.
2.
3.

DAY 9

Today, I am grateful for:

1.
2.
3.

EXERCISE (CONT.)

	MORNING	EVENING
DAY 10 *Today, I am grateful for:*	1.	
	2.	
	3.	
DAY 11 *Today, I am grateful for:*	1.	
	2.	
	3.	

	MORNING	EVENING
DAY 12 *Today, I am grateful for:*	1. 2. 3.	
DAY 13 *Today, I am grateful for:*	1. 2. 3.	

 **EXERCISE (CONT.)**

	MORNING	EVENING
DAY 14 *Today, I am grateful for:*	1. 2. 3.	
DAY 15 *Today, I am grateful for:*	1. 2. 3.	

	MORNING	EVENING

DAY 16

Today, I am grateful for:

1.

2.

3.

DAY 17

Today, I am grateful for:

1.

2.

3.

 **EXERCISE (CONT.)**

	MORNING	EVENING
DAY 18 *Today, I am grateful for:*	1. 2. 3.	
DAY 19 *Today, I am grateful for:*	1. 2. 3.	

	MORNING	EVENING

DAY 20

Today, I am grateful for:

1.

2.

3.

DAY 21

Today, I am grateful for:

1.

2.

3.

EXERCISE (CONT.)

	MORNING	EVENING
DAY 22 *Today, I am grateful for:*	1. 2. 3.	
DAY 23 *Today, I am grateful for:*	1. 2. 3.	

	MORNING	EVENING

DAY 24

Today, I am grateful for:

1.

2.

3.

DAY 25

Today, I am grateful for:

1.

2.

3.

EXERCISE (CONT.)

	MORNING	EVENING
DAY 26 *Today, I am grateful for:*	1. 2. 3.	
DAY 27 *Today, I am grateful for:*	1. 2. 3.	

	MORNING	EVENING
DAY 28 Today, I am grateful for:	1. 2. 3.	
DAY 29 Today, I am grateful for:	1. 2. 3.	

EXERCISE (CONT.)

	MORNING	EVENING
DAY 30 Today, I am grateful for:	1.	
	2.	
	3.	
DAY 31 Today, I am grateful for:	1.	
	2.	
	3.	

07 UTILISATION

CHAPTER 7:
UTILISATION

> *They did not know it was impossible so they did it."*
>
> – Mark Twain

This final and incredibly important secret habit refers to your ability to take anything and everything that happens and utilise it for your advantage and success. I draw a massive distinction here between 'using' situations, or people and utilising. This isn't about taking advantage *of* others for your own benefit. Rather, I mean to find the positive angle or leverage point to any situation, incident or occurrence and work with and through it to assist you to move forward.

The father of modern Hypnosis, Milton Erickson was renowned for his ability to turn anything to the advantage of his work with his patients. He might be in the middle of a therapy appointment and someone walked in opening the door to his office. In the past, another hypnotherapist would have a stop to the hypnosis session blaming the opening of the door for distracting his patient and thereby breaking the hypnotic trance. Erickson, on the other hand simply said something to the patient like, "even now you will notice *new doors* of opportunity *opening* in your mind". The patient would simply accept the real sound and the hypnotic suggestion, taking them both on board to create an even more powerful experience.

I teach Speakers, Presenters and Trainers to do exactly the same thing. If something unexpected occurs during a presentation, incorporate it into their presentation and utilise it to theirs and their audience's benefit. It could be something as simple as making a humorous reference all the way to enfolding the actual event into the lessons of the day. At my most advanced Master Trainer Training level we spend the best part of a day working on developing the capacity in the new Master Trainers to (what I call) abstract and adapt the everyday occurrences of life to enhance the lessons for their Students.

The only way to learn how to use the power of utilisation is to begin using it. Begin to look at the things happening around you and ask yourself a different set of questions:

- **What is good about this?**
- **What else can this mean?**
- **How does this help me create my goals, improve my performance, achieve better results?**

APPENDIX

SUCCESS

- FOCUS ON YOUR OUTCOME
- UTILISATION
- INNER GAME OF EVERYTHING
- DECISIONS
- FLEX-ABILITY
- AWARENESS & ATTENTION
- STRATEGIC ACTION

three days to focus
on making the next year of your life
the best year of your life so far

| MINDSET | STRATEGY | ACTION | RESULT |

Life AND Destiny PRIVATE RETREAT

During the *Life & Destiny Private Retreat*, I will lead you through discovering exactly what will increase the passion, power and excitement in your life. I will help you to determine precisely which goals and achievements will turn the next 12 months into your best 12 months ever.

Then, you will learn how to make your goals come alive. Real life tested and tried strategies and tactics will help you in taking the time you need, gaining the focus you want and creating the life you will love in order to achieve and succeed.

The retreat is held exclusively for only 10 people at a time in an ideal mountain location that works perfectly to enhance the experience.

want to know more?
Click here for information on The Life & Destiny Private Retreat.

DUANEALLEY.COM/LIFE-DESTINY-RETREAT/

Duane Alley TRAINING

Simple steps to survive the stressful situations of everyday life

Learn how to notice and fight the signs of burnout and the blues even before they take hold!

GET A COPY OF THE BOOK

for yourself or a friend in need of guidance!

www.DuaneAlley.com

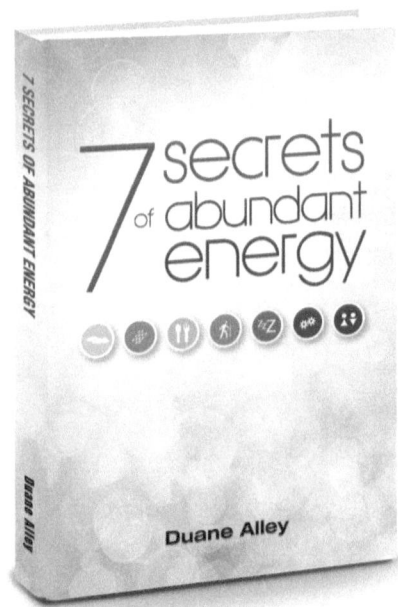 

GET THE COMPLETE 7 SECRETS SERIES!

VISIT DUANE ALLEY TRAINING ONLINE STORE:

www.DuaneAlley.com

www.ingramcontent.com/pod-product-compliance
Lightning Source LLC
Chambersburg PA
CBHW022019290426
44109CB00015B/1236